THE
TWILIGHT
BOYS

Inside Out

THE TWILIGHT BOYS

Inside · Out

MEL WILLIAMS

Piccadilly Press • London

MEET THE
TWILIGHT BOYS

Watch out, world – a new constellation of male Hollywood stars is sizzling on big screens across the globe. The deep-eyed vampires and hot-blooded werewolves of the *Twilight* saga movies are irresistibly multi-talented, mega-charming, and muscled to perfection!

But are the actors who play these buff supernatural beings as sensational in real life as they are on-screen? Are they honestly high-kicking martial arts heroes? Do they really hang out together during their down time? Is Bella Swan actually their ideal girl? This book will tell you what the *Twilight* boys are really like, inside and out . . .

Meet Edward Cullen

Is Edward Cullen the most DROP-DEAD gorgeous and desirable vampire ever to hit the big screen? In the *Twilight* saga, Edward falls in love with Bella Swan, a human teenager. Edward sees himself as a monster – but who wouldn't strongly disagree? Apart from being 'inhumanly beautiful', he is gentlemanly, has many talents, and is so caring that he would rather sacrifice his own happiness than put Bella in danger.

It may be hard to believe, but when it was first announced that Robert Pattinson was cast as Edward in the movies, there was a storm of protest from fans of the books – Rob wasn't at all what they had in mind. However as soon as trailers from *Twilight* were screened, the fans went from moaning to swooning! Now it's hard to imagine Edward being played by anyone else. Director Catherine Hardwicke has said: 'I feel like a genius to have chosen him for the part.' Author Stephenie Meyer has commented: 'There are very few actors who can look both dangerous and beautiful at the same time . . .'

QUICK QUIZ

Q) Who is Robert's favourite ever vampire?

A) He likes the original Nosferatu, Max Schreck.

Fast fact

In Rob's audition for *Twilight*, when he had only just met co-star Kristen Stewart (already cast as Bella), he had to act out a love scene on director Catherine Hardwicke's own bed!

A biography with bite!

Nicknames:	Rob, RPattz, Spunk Ransom
Birth:	13 May 1986 in London, England
Star signs:	Western zodiac – Taurus, Chinese zodiac - Tiger
Height:	6 foot 1 inch / 185 cm
Eyes:	Blue-grey (and dreamy!)
Family:	Mum – Clare (used to work in a model agency), Dad – Richard (importer of American cars), two sisters – Elizabeth (3 years older than Rob, a singer-songwriter) and Victoria (5 years older than Rob, works in advertising)
Pets:	Rob used to have a beloved dog named Patty
Childhood:	Grew up in Barnes, London. Loved music – played piano from age 3, guitar from age 5.
School:	Sent to private schools. Well-liked, but didn't try hard, never got good grades and often naughty. Was actually expelled at 12, though no one knows why!
Idols:	At the age of 13 watched the movie *One Flew Over the Cuckoo's Nest* and ever since has looked up to actor Jack Nicholson.
Start in acting:	At 15, joined the Barnes Theatre Company, to get to know some girls he had seen in a burger bar. At first worked behind the scenes but soon tried acting and was hooked. First role was a tiny part as a Cuban dancer in the musical *Guys and Dolls!* After a couple of lead roles, was 'spotted' by a theatrical agent and signed up. First professional part was in a TV movie called *The Ring of the Nibelungs*. Then won the role of Cedric Diggory in *Harry Potter and the Goblet of Fire* – and the rest is history . . .

Rob's vampire credentials

Edward is described by Bella as being 'impossibly beautiful'.

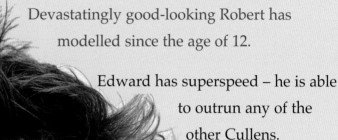

Devastatingly good-looking Robert has modelled since the age of 12.

Edward has superspeed – he is able to outrun any of the other Cullens.

Rob is not a natural at sports and has said 'I look like a duck when I run'. But after having serious personal training programmes for the stunts and strenuous physical scenes in *Harry Potter* and *Twilight*, his ripped body speaks for itself.

Edward is very musical – expert at playing the piano. He loves all music, from rock to classical.

Rob is passionate about music. He once formed a rock band called Bad Girls with friends, and writes and performs his own songs under the name Bobby Dupea. Two of his songs 'Never Think' and 'Let Me Sign', are on the *Twilight* soundtrack.

Edward is intensely private and mysterious.

Robert is intensely private and mysterious too. He lives mostly in hotel rooms because he travels so much and he doesn't even let the maids in to clean! After all, his room is the only place he gets any time and space to himself. Fans wait for him all the time and follow him everywhere . . .

Edward can read the mind of anyone within a few miles – except Bella . . .

Can Robert read minds? If you are ever lucky enough to have him gaze deep into your eyes, perhaps you will find out . . .

R Pattz vital statz

Rob is not just a pretty face. His impressive acting CV lists: • King of Scotland in Shakespeare's *Macbeth*

• A romantic villain in a theatre version of *Tess of the d'Urbervilles*

• A disabled man in TV movie *The Haunted Airman*

• Social misfit in comedy film *How to Be*

• Gay Spanish artist Salvador Dali in *Little Ashes*

QUICK QUIZ

Q) What did Robert sell at a charity auction at the Cannes Film Festival in 2009?

A) Two kisses – £17,500 for EACH smooch!

- An ambitious journalist in 19th century Paris in *Bel Ami*
- Adopted Commanche Indian in *Unbound Captives* (unreleased)

The many awards and accolades Rob has won include:

Breakthrough Male Performance and Best Kiss (MTV 2009)

Male Hottie (Teen Choice 2009)

Best Actor in a Feature (Strasbourg International Film Festival 2008)

one of the 'Sexiest Men Alive' (*People* magazine, 2008 and 2009)

one of *Vanity Fair* magazine's 'Top Hollywood Earners of 2009' ($18million)

'Best Dressed Man of 2010' by *GQ* magazine

Let's get personal . . .

- Rob isn't materialistic – he says: 'The only thing I've really bought is my car, which cost $1,500 and keeps exploding.
- 'I wear the same clothes every day . . .'
- His best mates are two friends he has had since he was 12.
- He can't stand girls wearing Uggs.
- He insists he's never dumped a girl, he's always the one that's dumped.
- He loves YouTube, *X Factor* and *American Idol*.
- Rob not only starred in, but also executively produced *Remember Me*.
- He wants to direct and write too.

Robert says . . .

On his career: 'The acting's come along by accident. I've never trained or anything . . .'

On becoming famous overnight, after *Harry Potter in* 2005: 'The day before, I was just sitting in Leicester Square, happily being ignored by everyone. Then suddenly strangers are screaming your name. Amazing!'

On the mass hysteria of thousands of fans at the British premiere of *Twilight* (described by the press as 'like Beatlemania with fangs!': 'It's absolutely mad – but they're here for the character, not for me.' (Rob is very modest.)

On the character of Edward Cullen: 'The thing I found interesting is that he is essentially the hero of the story but violently denies he is the hero.'

On being the star of the worldwide phenomenon that is *Twilight*: 'It's kind of terrifying in a lot of ways. I still can't come to terms with it.'

On the pressures of being one of the most adored men on the planet: 'I spend a lot of time trying to figure out how not to be seen.'

On on-and-off-screen relationship with Kristen Stewart: 'She's a unique girl. You really don't meet many people like Kristen.'

Hollywood hot property Kellan Lutz plays Emmett – Edward's super-strong brother, who is first wary of Bella but warms to her. Kellan has said: 'Emmett's awesome. He's the coolest character . . . He's the fun-loving vampire.'

Meet

Emmett Cullen

Nickname: 'Crazy Kellan' because when he was little he used to go nuts when he lost his temper

Birth: 15 March 1985 in Dickinson, North Dakota, USA

Family: 7 brothers and 1 sister – Kellan is fourth

Pets: Kellan has two cherished dogs

Start in acting: Kellan acted first in church plays, then the high school drama society. He modelled from 13. He moved to LA to study chemical engineering at university, but instead modelled in a high-profile Abercrombie & Fitch advertising campaign. He then began auditioning successfully for TV shows such as *Heroes* and *90210*, and movies including *Prom Night* and *Deep Winter* before Emmett

Likes: Horror movies, peanut butter, John Grisham novels, doing stunts

Vampire credentials

Emmett is very tall and muscular.

Kellan is a 6 foot 1 inch (185.5cm) trained athlete. He bulked up more for Emmett through exercise and diet.

Emmett is extremely competitive.

Kellan lives to compete at extreme skateboarding, weight-training, athletics, baseball, tennis, basketball, lacrosse, swimming, badminton, skiing, snowboarding, dance, Nintendo Wii . . . you get the picture.

Emmett loves teasing people and playing jokes.

Kellan enjoyed playing pranks on the *Twilight* cast and crew with Peter Facinelli (Carlisle Cullen).

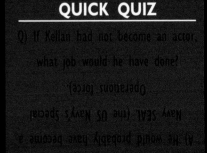

QUICK QUIZ

Q) If Kellan had not become an actor, what job would he have done?

A) He would probably have become a Navy SEAL (the US Navy's special Operations force).

THE VAMPIRES

Meet Jasper Hale

One of Kellan Lutz's off-screen friends plays his on-screen brother – the beautiful Jackson Rathbone is Jasper Hale, a vampire who can manipulate emotions and struggles not to feed on humans.

Birth: 21 December 1984, Singapore

Family: Sisters Ryann and Kelly (older) and Brittany (younger). Father had a job which moved the family around the world to places like Indonesia and Norway.

Start in acting: Jackson began performing musical theatre with a local group, the Pickwick Players. He then majored in acting at high school. He intended to go on to study acting at college, but instead went to Hollywood to try his luck. He scored roles in TV shows like *The O.C.* and *The Valley of Light* before making it onto the big screen in a couple of films and landing the role of Jasper.

Likes: Music (he performs in a band called 100 Monkeys), writing and producing. Fave actors include Christopher Walken, Clint Eastwood, Robert Downey Jr., Katharine Hepburn and River Phoenix.

Vampire credentials

Jasper is extremely charismatic.

An interviewer for MTV once described Jackson as more charismatic than George Clooney.

Jasper used to be a southern Confederate soldier in the American Civil War.

Jackson used to live in the southern state of Texas and took Texas History classes to learn about the Civil War.

Jasper has to stay out of the sun, to prevent his vampire nature being revealed.

Jackson told a reporter once, 'I'm not really a sun person . . . I live during the night.'

Jackson says . . .

'I used to want to be a vampire when I was young.'

Meet Carlise Cullen

Peter says . . .

'I read Twilight right before I met with Catherine Hardwicke. I read the book in one day; I couldn't put it down. It was fantastic.'

Peter Facinelli has won hearts everywhere as compassionate Carlisle Cullen, born in 1640s London, England.

Birth: 26 November 1973 in Queens, New York

Family: The son of Italian immigrants to the US, he is married to the *90210* actress Jennie Garth, with whom he has three daughters.

Acting career: Knew from age 8 that he wanted to be an actor, but had to overcome being very shy. Studied acting at New York University's Tisch School of the Arts. Has played roles in top TV shows such as *Six Feet Under*, *Damages* and *Nurse Jackie*, and movies including *Riding in Cars with Boys* and *The Scorpion King*. He has worked alongside top talents including Jennifer Love-Hewitt, Drew Barrymore, Christian Slater and Matthew Broderick.

Likes: Playing non-Italian roles, or he doesn't feel he's acting. And his favourite vampire is the Count from *Sesame Street*!

Vampire credentials

Carlisle is the adoptive father of the Olympic vampire coven.

Peter is around ten years older than most of the other Cullens, plus he has three children, so it wasn't hard for him to play the father role.

Carlisle has had 300 years honing medical skills as a doctor.

Peter had medical training so he could play the role of a skilled doctor convincingly.

THE VAMPIRES

Meet James

Cam Gigandet appears only in the first instalment of the saga, *Twilight* (sigh!). As human-blood-drinker James, he obsesses about Bella and hunts her down before being destroyed by Emmett, Jasper and Alice.

Full name: Cameron Joslin Gigandet

Birth: 16 August 1982 in Tacoma, Washington, USA

Family: Parents, Jay and Kim Gigandet, and sister, Kelsie. He and his girlfriend, Dominique Geisendorff had a daughter in 2009.

Start in acting: After being an American football quarterback in high school, he attended Santa Monica Community College in California, took an acting class and fell in love with it. First role was on TV crime drama *CSI*. Also a regular on *The O.C.* before a couple of movie roles led to the part of James. Several movie lead roles since, including in *Never Back Down*, about a high school boy lured into an underground fight club.

Likes: Basketball, golf, skiing, surfing and Krav Maga (a self-defence system)

Vampire credentials

In *Twilight*, James is a very talented tracker.

Cam's tracking skills only extend as far as house-hunting with his girlfriend.

James is an extremely skilled fighter.

Cam won MTV's Movie Awards' Best Fight – twice! (Once with Robert Pattinson for *Twilight*, and also with Sean Faris in *Never Back Down*.) He also has a black belt in the martial art of Krav Maga.

QUICK QUIZ

Q) What colour are vampire eyes?

A) The animal-blood-drinking vampires of the Olympic coven have golden eyes which darken to black as they thirst. Human-blood-drinkers have burgundy eyes which darken.

23

Meet Alec

Alec is a member of powerful Italian vampire coven, the Volturi, the law enforcers of the vampire world. He appears for the first time in *New Moon*, played in the movie by the boy with cherub looks, Cameron Bright.

Real name: Cameron Douglas Crigger

Birth: 26 January 1993 in Victoria, Canada

Family: Mother, Anne. (His parents divorced when he was two.) Older brother Bryce Nelson (also an actor).

Start in acting: At an early age, Cameron was often mistaken for Jake Lloyd, the child actor who played Anakin Skywalker in *Star Wars: The Phantom Menace*. So his mother signed him to a casting agency aged 6 and, soon after, he got his first acting job in a TV commercial. He had acting lessons at Spotlight Academy, and gained several roles in TV shows such as *Dark Angel*. Has played in movies since age 11, such as *The Butterfly Effect*, *Juno*, and *X-Men: The Last Stand* (as Leech). Has worked alongside movie stars including Robert de Niro, Mila Jovovich, Hugh Jackman and Halle Berry.

Likes: Cars. Cameron wants to go to college to learn how to be a motor mechanic!

Vampire credentials

Stephenie Meyer's invention of the Volturi has provoked controversy because 'purist' fans think that vampires shouldn't have unusual aspects such as 'royal families', and glittering skin.

Cameron is no stranger to controversy. In *Birth*, he shared a kiss and a bath scene with Nicole Kidman. He says, 'Vampires don't exist! We can portray them any way we want to.'

Cameron says . . .

'I'm friends with all the wolf pack. If I were Bella, I'd go with Jacob!'

25

Meet Jacob Black

Edward Cullen is Bella's true love in *Twilight*, but in the second instalment of the saga, *New Moon*, he abandons her to the charms of a tall, dark and handsome rival – Jacob Black, who brings a whole new meaning to 'animal magnetism'. Jacob is a Native American of the Quileute tribe, a descendant of an ancient line of 'shape-shifters' that assume wolf form. Alas, the Quileutes are also the mortal enemies of vampires . . . In the third and fourth instalments of the saga, *Eclipse* and *Breaking Dawn*, can Edward and Jacob reconcile their differences or are they doomed to be sworn rivals for ever?

Rising star Taylor Lautner bagged the coveted role of Jacob without knowing what he was getting himself into – he hadn't read the best-selling novels or heard that *Twilight* was an obsession worldwide. When he realised what a daunting responsibility playing Jacob was, he told a reporter: 'It's hard not to be nervous when you know there's a few million [*Twilight*] fans out there who are just dying for this movie to come out . . .'

Fast fact

When Taylor auditioned for *Twilight*, Kristen and Robert had already been cast as Bella and Edward. Taylor had to read scenes with Kristen to see if they had chemistry and to prove he had the looks and acting ability to rival Robert's irresistible vampire!

The Lautner Life Story

Nicknames: Taylor Daniel Lautner

Birth: 11 February 1992 in Grand Rapids, Michigan, USA

Star signs: Western zodiac – Aquarius, Chinese zodiac - Monkey

Height: 5 foot 10 inches / 178 cm

Eyes: Deep brown – like chocolate!

Family: Mum – Deborah (an office worker), Dad – Daniel (an airline pilot), one sister, younger by 6 years – Makena

Pets: A Maltese dog named Roxy

Childhood: Became mad on watching and playing all sorts of sport as a toddler. Began karate lessons at age 6 and a year later won three first-place trophies in a national competition. Was invited by world karate champion and TV's Blue Power Ranger Mike Chat to attend regular training sessions in LA for 'extreme martial arts', or XMA. By the age of 8, was a karate black belt, gold medallist at the World Karate Association Championships, and was competing and performing in the XMA elite squad. Was also a straight A-grader at school. Phew!

Start in acting: Mike Chat helped Taylor get a theatrical agent, so whenever Taylor was in LA, he would go for auditions. At 9, he won his first role: a part in a martial arts action movie for TV, *Shadow Fury*. Taylor was bitten by the showbiz bug, and the Lautners moved to LA so he could pursue his dreams of Hollywood stardom . . .

QUICK QUIZ

Q) What is Taylor's worst habit?

A) Wiggling his knee all the time when he's sitting down.

29

TAYLOR

Shaping up as a shape-shifter

Jacob is a member of the ancient shape-shifting Quileute tribe of Native Americans.

Taylor has Native American heritage. He is part Potawatomi and Ottawa Indian onhis mother's side.

Between *Twilight* and *New Moon*, Jacob undergoes extreme physical changes as he matures and develops the ability to shape-shift into a giant wolf. He goes from a lanky 6ft 2 inches to 6ft 7 inches of rippling muscle.

After *Twilight*, Taylor embarked on an intensive weight-training and diet plan to pack an incredible 30 pounds of muscle onto his lean, athletic frame.

Jacob is usually a happy person who can cheer those around him, but when he's angered – watch out!

Taylor has said: 'The first movie shows you [Jacob's] regular boyish side. That side is just like me, he's talkative and fun. In the second book . . . he's totally opposite. That challenges me as an actor.'

Jacob can execute incredible physical feats of speed and strength.

Taylor can execute incredible physical feats. Have you seen his upside down splits where he balances on one hand?

Jacob has the superpower of being able to communicate telepathically with his wolf pack when in wolf form.

Taylor has said that he would like X-ray vision like Superman.

The Low-down on Lautner

A talent on TV – Before hitting the big screen, Taylor guest-starred in many comedies and dramas and was also in great demand as a voiceover artist for cartoons and advertisements.

Making it in movies – Taylor's first leading role in a movie was at age 13, showing off his martial arts skills as superhero Sharkboy in *The Adventures of Sharkboy and Lavagirl*. He then appeared in *Cheaper by the Dozen 2* with comedy legend Steve Martin before landing the role of Jacob Black.

Brains as well as beefcake – While filming *Twilight*, 16-year-old Taylor took his high school tests early, on set. He now carries his laptop everywhere because he is taking an online college psychology degree course.

The boy next door – Taylor's parents used to keep him on a budget, so he learned the value of money. He has many showbiz mates, but he is just as likely to hang out with his old school friends. He relaxes by playing baseball, basketball, football or soccer, or going swimming or riding – if you can call all that relaxation!

Lautner loves . . . The colour blue, steak with A1 sauce and cake batter flavour ice cream, movie *The Last Samurai*, movie stars Denzel Washington, Brad Pitt and Matt Damon, TV shows *American Idol* and *The Apprentice*, pop group Black Eyed Peas, and Mexican and Chinese food.

Taylor says . . .

On childhood: 'I was never extremely confident. Because I was an actor, when I was in school, there was a little bullying going on.'

On trying to get into the acting business: 'The average booking rate when you're starting is one out of seventy-five auditions . . . You just can't get down and quit . . . it's very, very difficult.'

On being part of the *Twilight* saga phenomenon: 'It's extremely cool . . .'

On the adoration of 'Team Jacob' fans: 'They're just passionate for the series and for the characters . . . I don't think it has much to do with me personally; it's more because I'm playing the beloved Jacob Black.' (No, Taylor, not exactly!)

On bulking up for *New Moon*: 'The hardest thing for me was the eating. I had to shove as much food in my body as possible to pack on calories. My trainer wanted me to do six meals a day and not go two hours without eating. If I would cheat on eating one day, I could tell – I'd drop a few pounds.'

On friendship: 'You gotta remember who your friends were before you got famous.'

On girlfriends: 'I think a girl is most attractive when wearing sweats and just being herself.'

Kristen Stewart on Taylor . . . 'I love that kid, I would do anything for that kid.'

QUICK QUIZ

Q) Taylor enjoyed watching American college football — which team did he support?

A) The Michigan Wolverines.

Meet *Meet* Embry Call

Embry Call is Jacob Black's best friend. His character is quiet and shy – but it's impossible not to notice Kiowa Gordon, who portrays him in the movies *New Moon* and *Eclipse*.

Birth: 25 March 1990 in Berlin, though he grew up in Arizona, USA

Family: Kiowa is part of the Hualapi Nation of Native Americans. His mother, Camille Nighthorse Gordon is also an actress. Kiowa is the seventh of eight children.

Start in acting: Kiowa goes to the same church as Stephenie Meyer. Stephenie approached him one day at a service, because she thought he would be perfect as a member of the wolf pack. Kiowa then went to an open casting call where, from thousands of hopefuls, he landed the part of Embry and established himself as a movie talent to watch.

Likes: Having long hair – he had to have it cut to play one of the wolf pack. Singing – Kiowa also works as a vocalist.

Shaping up as a shape-shifter

Embry is more reserved than the other wolf pack boys.

Fans who have been lucky enough to meet Kiowa at *Twilight* conventions and personal appearances find him to be shy and self-conscious.

Embry is playful.

Kiowa always messes about with photographers. He strikes amusing poses when he is spotted by paparazzi.

Kiowa says . . .
*'We bonded really well.
The wolf pack – we're
like brothers now.'*

Meet Quil Ateara

Jacob Black's second cousin, Quil Ateara, may lack a certain smoothness with the ladies – but thousands of fans have been charmed by Tyson Houseman, who plays him.

Birth: 9 February 1990 in Edmonton, Canada

Family: Tyson is a Native American of the Cree Nation. He has three younger brothers.

Start in acting: While at the Victoria School of the Visual and Performing Arts in Edmonton, he performed in several plays, including Romeo in Shakespeare's *Romeo and Juliet*. The first audition Tyson ever went to was an open casting call – all he knew was that it was for 'a major motion picture'. It turned out to be *New Moon*. Tyson then got an acting agent and his career has been rocketing ever since . . .

Likes: Snowboarding, skateboarding and guitar. Tyson has been excellent at art since he was little and he loves drawing, painting and photography.

Shaping up as a shape-shifter

Quil comes late to join the wolf pack, so has a different bonding experience to the others.

In *New Moon*, Tyson had a different shooting schedule and costume work to the other shapeshifter actors. He was friends with the rest of the guys, but he didn't get to spend loads of time with them until filming *Eclipse*.

Tyson on his co-stars . . .
'Kiowa – witty. Alex – devoted. Bronson – funny.'

Taylor Lautner on Tyson . . .
'I loved shooting the scenes with Embry and Quil.'

Meet
Seth Clearwater

Seth Clearwater is the most free-thinking member of Jacob Black's crew of shape-shifters. Some fans dare to think that Boo Boo Stewart, who plays him, has even better abs than Taylor Lautner!

Real name: Nils Allen Stewart Jnr.

Birth: 21 January 1994 in Beverley Hills, California

Family: Father, Nils Allen Stewart Snr., mother Renee, three sisters: Trent 'Fivel', Maegan and Sage. From his mother's side he is Japanese, Chinese and Korean, and from his father's side he is Scottish, Russian and Blackfoot Native American.

Start in acting: Boo Boo has been acting, singing, dancing and modelling since little. He was a world champion martial artist by the age of ten. He has performed with Miley Cyrus, the Jonas Brothers and done stunt-double work on films including *Beowulf* with Angelina Jolie, and has appeared in several TV shows and movies before and since *Twilight*. His star is certainly rising – and fast . . .

Likes: Rock music and wrestling. Boo Boo has pictures of himself with various WWE stars on his official MySpace page, attends major wrestling events such as Summerslam, and has written for the TNA Wrestling website.

Shaping up as a shape-shifter

Seth is close to his sister, Leah Clearwater, who is the only female shape-shifter in the *Twilight* saga.

Boo Boo is close to his sisters too. With Fivel and Maegan, he songwrites and performs in a band.

QUICK QUIZ

Q) Why did Stephenie Meyer use the name Seth?

A) It's her brother's name.

Meet Paul

Paul is a shape-shifter prone to episodes of rage where he bursts into his wolf form. He is played by piercing-eyed performer, Alex Meraz.

Birth: 10 January 1985 in Mesa, Arizona

Family: Alex is a Native Mexican Indian from the Purepecha tribe. With his Vietnamese-American wife, Kim, he has a son named Somak.

Career: Although Alex studied acting in high school, he wanted to be a professional painter. He attended the New School for the Arts and afterwards worked as a teacher of all sorts of arts from mask-making to break dance. He then specialised as a performer of indigenous dance, founding a group called Dancing Earth. Friend and mentor Raoul Trujillo saw him dance and encouraged him to try acting. Alex's first big film role was a warrior in *New World*, alongside megastar Colin Farrell.

Likes: Alex studied mixed martial arts for ten years, winning many karate and capoeira tournaments. He loves performing his own stunts.

Shaping up as a shape-shifter

In *New Moon*, Jacob says that Paul is shorter than him and not as beefy as Quil.

The first day Alex met Taylor, he overheard him ask Edi Gathegi [the vampire Laurent] if he was bigger than him. Edi answered, 'He's just wider'. Alex teased him about overhearing it and from there they became gym buddies and shared workout tips.

Fast fact

Alex takes studying for acting roles very seriously. However, hard work couldn't help him win a part in Mel Gibson's movie *Apocalypto* – he was turned down because he didn't look Mayan enough.

Meet Jared

Jared was the third shapeshifter to join the pack, and is played by Bronson Pelletier, who would rather be a shape-shifter than a vampire any time. He has said: 'We're wild, we're one with nature. It's great. We can be in human form one second and – boom! Become a wolf, just like that, if the mood strikes!'

Birth: 31 December 1986 (New Year's Eve!) in Canada

Family: Bronson is a French-Canadian of Plains Cree and Metis Native American descent. He has four brothers. His mother calls herself 'an unpaid referee'.

Career: Bronson was a struggling actor before *Twilight*, he had parts in movies *Art Zone* and *Dinosapien*, but was best known for his role as Jack Sinclair in *renegadepress.com*.

QUICK QUIZ

Q)What happened when Bronson was once playing football off-set with the wolf pack?

A) His shoe flew off and hit Tyson Houseman in the face — Tyson had to go back to the make-up trailer to get all the dirt off his face and have his make-up redone.

Likes: Bronson loves listening to punk rock and rap and playing video games.

Shaping up as a shape-shifter

The pack members are as close as brothers.

Bronson has four brothers, so he's used to all the intense ups and downs of living in a pack.

The wolf pack are fantastically fast, strong and one of few creatures able to destroy a vampire.

Bronson has always wanted to be a werewolf since watching the movie *Underworld*.

Bronson says . . .

'I'm really honoured to be part of such a huge project.'

BREAKING DAWN

It's hard to imagine *Twilight* coming to an end, so it's good news that the fourth instalment in the saga, *Breaking Dawn*, may well be made into not just one movie, but two! Even better, there will be many more beautiful actors called on to play new, sultry vampire characters, as members of various covens from around the world are called together, and the brooding Jacob will be flanked by his entire hunksome wolf pack. Of course, Robert Pattinson and Taylor Lautner are signed to reprise their roles. After all, it's impossible to imagine Edward and Jacob played by anyone else!

Fast fact

The actors who play the shape-shifters have talked about all getting the special wolf pack tattoo for real, so keep your eyes open . . .

QUICK QUIZ

Q) How might the half-vampire, half-human baby Renesmee be portrayed in *Breaking Dawn?*

A) By CGI special effects, like the creatures in the movie *Avatar.*

Only the beginning . . .

So, what does the future hold for these hot actors after the final *Twilight* saga movies finally wrap for good? Well, their stars are not so much rising as rocketing. As well as already having filmed several new starring roles, Robert Pattinson has been Executive Producer on the 2010 flick *Remember Me* and has revealed his secret ambition to play James Bond one day. You can see equally-in-demand rival, Taylor Lautner, starring in rom-com *Valentine's Day*, thriller *Abduction*, and martial arts action movie *Stretch Armstrong*. The other gorgeous *Twilight* boys are hard on their heels – just watch this space!

First published in Great Britain in 2010 by Piccadilly Press Ltd,
5 Castle Road, London NW1 8PR www.piccadillypress.co.uk
Designed by Simon Davis. Printed and bound in Italy by Printer Trento srl   ISBN: 978 1 84812 110 2

1 3 5 7 9 10 8 6 4 2